I have
EPILEPSY

I have
EPILEPSY

Brenda Pettenuzzo
meets
Salvatore Conte

Consultants: The British Epilepsy Association

Photography: Chris Fairclough

FRANKLIN WATTS

London/New York/Sydney/Toronto

Salvatore Conte is eleven years old. He has one brother, Eduardo, aged 13, and three sisters: Assunta, aged 15, Antonietta, aged 9, and Sandra, aged 5. Salvatore and his two younger sisters attend St Joachim's primary school. Assunta and Eduardo are at secondary school. His mother, Joanna, works in a cafe, and his father, Antonio, is a butcher. The family live in the London Docklands.

Contents

© 1989 Franklin Watts
96–98 Leonard Street
LONDON EC2

ISBN: 0 863138705

Series Consultant: Beverley Mathias
Editor: Jenny Wood
Design: K & Co

Typesetting: Keyspools Ltd

Printed in Great Britain

The Publishers, Photographer and Author would like to thank Salvatore Conte and his family for their great help and co-operation in the preparation of this book.

Thanks are also due to St Joachim's Primary School and to the British Epilepsy Association.

Brenda Pettenuzzo is a science and religious education teacher at St Angela's Ursuline Convent School, a comprehensive school in the London Borough of Newham.

The first signs

"I didn't have epilepsy when I was a baby, and no-one in my family has ever had fits."

Salvatore was born in Italy, and came to England when he was eighteen months old. He had a normal birth and was a "normal" baby in every way. Anybody can start to have epileptic fits, and just like most other people with epilepsy, there is nothing in Salvatore's medical history to explain why he should have them.

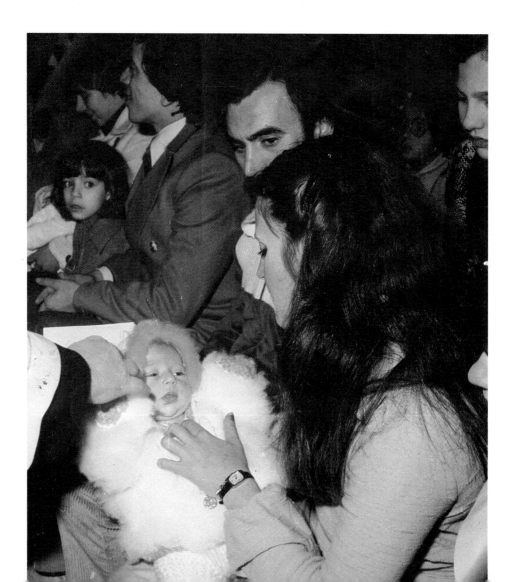

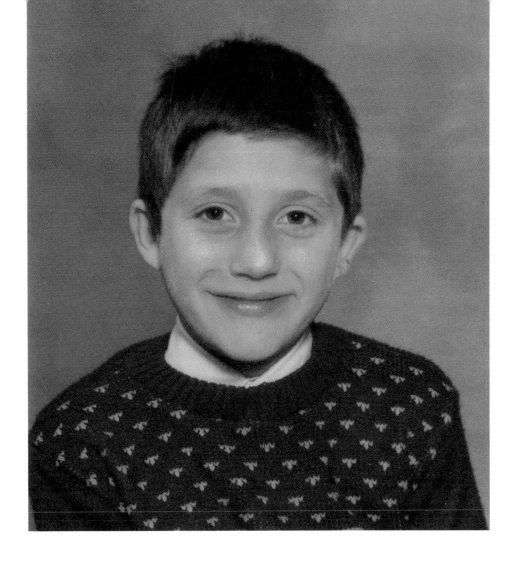

"I had my first fit when I was nine. I was playing with some friends and they ran to tell my mum."

Salvatore's mother had noticed his head moving in an odd way once or twice. She had begun to wonder if he had a nervous twitch of some kind.

One day, Salvatore was playing with some friends near his house. His friends ran to tell his mum that he had fallen down and would not wake up. Salvatore's mother was very worried and as soon as he "came round" she took him to see the doctor.

Check-ups and tests

"I go to the hospital every three months for a check-up. First of all, I'm weighed and measured."

Every hospital check-up includes a general health check as well. The doctor needs to know that Salvatore's general health and development are good. He asks Salvatore about how he is feeling, and answers any questions he or his mum might have. The doctor also explains any changes he makes to Salvatore's medicine.

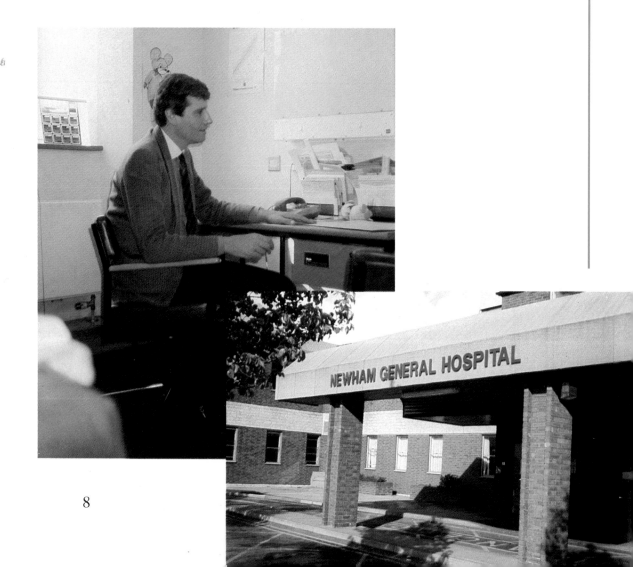

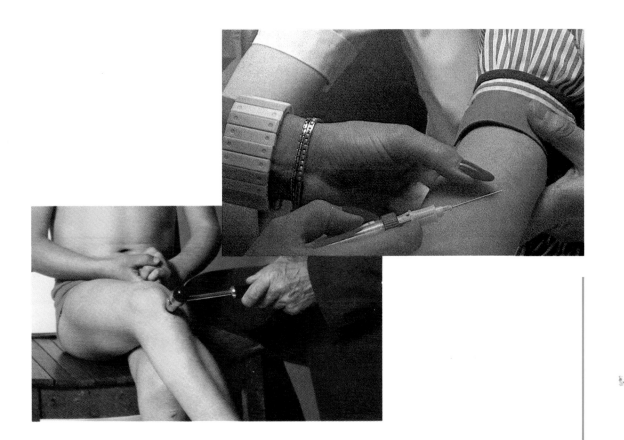

"The doctor tests my reflexes, and sometimes I have a blood test."

Reflexes are the automatic responses of certain nerves. Blinking and coughing are reflexes, and there are many others. Sometimes, when there is something wrong with the nervous system, the reflexes are affected. Doctors use them as an indicator of health. The amount of medicine in Salvatore's blood is checked with a blood test. It is important that Salvatore takes exactly the right amount of medicine. If he takes too little, his fits will not be properly controlled. The blood test helps the doctor to decide what dose he should prescribe.

9

"Sometimes the doctor sends me for other tests."

Most people with epilepsy will have an E.E.G. test at some time. This records the electrical activity occurring within the brain. Electrodes are placed on the scalp and the electrical activity is recorded on a graph and measured.

A person with epilepsy is likely to have a characteristic pattern of electrical activity. The doctor can often tell the type of epilepsy from this test.

Some people with epilepsy are also given a C.T. scan. This uses a special form of X-ray and a computer to show pictures of the electrical activity in different parts of the brain.

"I have to take special tablets. They act slowly all day, so I mustn't forget to take them."

Salvatore's tablets help to stop him having fits, but only if he takes them regularly. The doctor has told Salvatore and his parents how many he must take so that the right amount of medicine is always in his bloodstream. Salvatore takes his tablets with a large glass of water to make them easier to swallow.

Warning signals

"Sometimes I can tell if I'm going to have a fit. I feel strange, and I keep rubbing my head."

Salvatore's mother and father noticed him rubbing the front of his head before he had a fit. Sometimes he does this instead of having a fit, and sometimes it comes before the fit itself. Doctors call this type of fit a partial seizure. Some people have only one type of fit, but others, like Salvatore, have more than one kind.

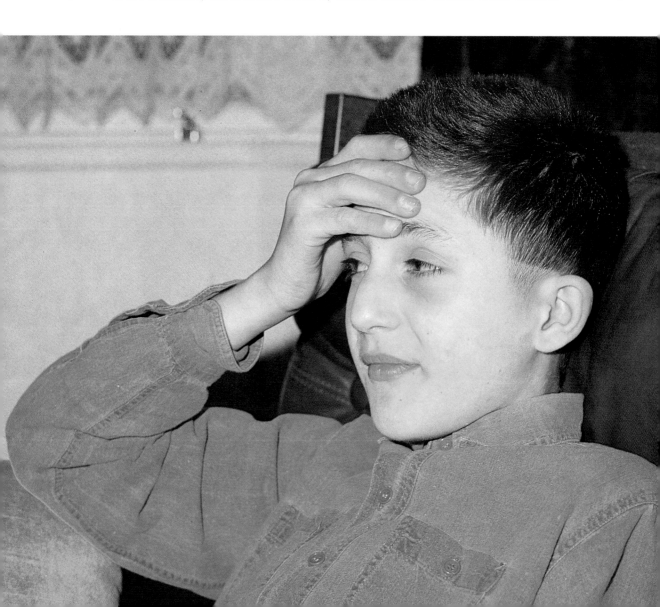

"I used to rub my head a lot while I was watching the television, but now I know how to avoid it."

Salvatore has found that he must not sit too close to the television screen as flashing lights can bring on a fit. Most doctors advise people with epilepsy to sit at least $2\frac{1}{2}$ metres away from the screen, and never to watch it in poor light. It is a good idea to have a small lamp on top of the television. When sitting close to the TV, many people find that covering one eye helps.

"When I have a fit, I don't know anything about it. It's as if I've been asleep."

A fit usually lasts for two or three minutes, but sometimes longer. Very rarely, Salvatore may have a really severe fit, and will have to go to hospital. Usually he is unconscious for a few minutes, his arms and legs may go stiff and jerk, and then he will "come round" again. His mum or dad waits with him until he wakes up, and then he has a short rest. After half an hour or so he feels better, but he cannot remember what has happened. Doctors call this type of fit a "tonic-clonic seizure".

At school

"My teacher knows that sometimes I have fits. I haven't had one in school, but if I did, he would know what to do."

Salvatore's mum told his school when he started to have fits. If he ever did have one while at school, they would know how to look after him, and they would call his mother at work if she was needed. The British Epilepsy Association publishes lots of information sheets which are useful for teachers whose pupils have epilepsy.

"I used to sit nearer to the window, but my teacher noticed the sun was in my eyes and changed my place."

Salvatore's fits are caused by several things. One cause is the sun. If the light is bright and it shines in his eyes, he may have a fit. He may just begin to "flick" his hand across his forehead. This is a warning sign. But sometimes, there are no warnings signs and he has a fit. Salvatore's teacher noticed that he was "flicking" his hand a lot when he sat near the window so he moved Salvatore's chair to a darker part of the classroom.

"We sometimes use a computer at school. I have to make sure I'm in front of the screen, but not too close."

VDU screens are safe for people with photo-sensitive epilepsy but Salvatore knows that if the screen is flickering, or if he is looking at it sideways, it might cause a problem. Watching a television screen is known to induce epilepsy in a few people but by trial and error, most people can find a safe way to watch. People who are sensitive to the television screen often find that flashing lights at discos can provoke fits too.

"When I play out at play time, I'm careful not to bang my head!"

Salvatore's parents worry about him when they aren't there to keep an eye on him. They know he is well supervised at school, but it is natural to worry. They do not think it would be a good idea to treat him very differently from other children, and as he gets older, he grows more responsible. He takes care not to do the things which might cause him to have a fit.

With the family

"I sometimes go swimming with my school, and sometimes with the family."

Many people worry that if their child has epilepsy it is dangerous to go swimming. There is always a risk when children are playing in water. If there is proper supervision, and a life guard at hand, then people with epilepsy are no more at risk than anyone else. Salvatore has never had a fit in the water but, just in case, he is never allowed to swim alone and someone is always at hand to help.

"I have a computer at home. My sister often plays games on it with me."

As usual, Salvatore sits in front of the screen to play. He doesn't play any games which flash or flicker too much. He also turns down the brightness on the monitor. Salvatore never plays with the computer alone. There is always someone with him, but that makes it more fun anyway!

"We have three pets, a dog, a cat, and a bird. I usually get the job of cleaning out the bird's cage."

For most children with epilepsy, the time they spend having seizures is only a tiny fraction of their lives. The rest of the time, they are perfectly normal, healthy children.

Sandra is the youngest in the family and to her, Salvatore is just a big brother. She has seen him having a fit, but her mum was there and in control of the situation and so Sandra wasn't frightened. She knows there is nothing to be frightened of.

"My dad loves his motorbike. I often help him wash it, but if I'm going out I usually go in the car with mum."

When he is old enough, Salvatore may be able to learn to drive. People who have had no fits while they have been awake for two years or more are allowed to drive. If Salvatore still has daytime fits when he is older, he will not be able to drive as it would be too dangerous. Perhaps by that time, he won't have any more fits, or he might only have them while he is asleep. It is quite common for children to grow out of their epilepsy as they get older.

"I have a bike, and I can ride it in the street, but only if there is someone nearby to watch me."

Salvatore's mum and dad don't think it would be very wise for him to cycle far from home on his own. He might have a fit and there would be no-one around to help him. They want him to do the things that other boys and girls do, but they have to keep an eye on him.

"I have three sisters, but Antonietta is the nearest to me in age. We do lots of things together."

There is only one school year between Salvatore and Antonietta, so they have a lot in common. They often go out to the local shop together. It is good for Salvatore to do this, and his mum and dad don't worry about him as they would if he wanted to go on his own.

"Sometimes my dad cooks, but usually my mum does it. We all help to get everything ready for dinner."

There are no special allowances made for Salvatore at home. Although his parents were quite shocked when they first learned that he had epilepsy, they knew that he would still be a normal boy in every way. In case he thinks there is anything special about him, Salvatore's sisters and brother are never far away to tell him otherwise! They see to it that he does his share of the chores.

"My mum is a good cook! We usually eat Italian food at home, but I love everything she makes!"

On Sundays, the whole family tries to have its main meal together. This isn't always possible when five children all want to do different things. Sunday lunch in the Conte household is similar to the meal they would be eating if they still lived in Italy. It starts with a large helping of pasta. When Salvatore and his family sit down to eat, he is no different from his brother or sisters. He is just like any other eleven year old boy.

Facts about epilepsy

Epilepsy takes its name from a Greek word which means to take hold of or seize. Epilepsy means to have fits or seizures which keep happening. Someone who has only had one fit would not be described as having epilepsy.

Epilepsy is the second most common disorder of the nervous system. The most common problem is migraine. Approximately 1 person in 200 is affected by epilepsy, and most of these have their first seizure before they are 20 years old.

Epilepsy affects people of any age, either sex, all races, and all degrees of intelligence. In some cases it is possible to identify the cause of the epilepsy, but in most the cause is not known. Sometimes the cause of epilepsy might be connected to a difficult birth, head injuries, a disease affecting the brain or other medical reasons. The fits or seizures themselves are the result of a biochemical disturbance in the brain. Epilepsy is not infectious, and is not a mental illness.

There are many types of fit. Some people have only one type, and others have several. No two people have exactly the same pattern of seizures, or the same pattern of recovery. If the whole brain is affected, then a person will have a "generalised" seizure. There are two main types of these. Some people have very brief generalised seizures called "absences". These last only a few seconds. The person looks blank, and may appear to have been daydreaming. He or she may be confused. This type of fit used to be called "petit mal" epilepsy. It is very important that any child with these "absences" is tested for epilepsy, as without treatment their lack of concentration can hold up progress at school. A tonic-clonic fit is the other well-known generalised seizure. It used to be called "grand mal" epilepsy. During a tonic-clonic fit, the person often stares oddly, before stiffening and falling down. They may cry out, and they usually have convulsions, or jerking movements of the body. After a few minutes, they usually return to normal, and regain consciousness. Some people can tell if they are going to have a fit. They feel or behave differently, and can try to make sure they are in a safe place if the fit is going to happen. You cannot stop someone having a fit once it has begun. The best "treatment" for someone having a tonic-clonic fit is to make them comfortable, cushion their head and protect them from injuring themselves. Do not try to force anything into the person's mouth. Once they are relaxed and the convulsion has stopped, they should be put in the recovery position, and someone should stay with them until they have fully recovered. After a fit such as this, different people have different after-effects. Some people find that they cannot remember what happened beforehand, some people have a headache or feel very tired. Although seizures like this can be very frightening for the onlooker, it is usually not necessary to call a doctor or ambulance unless the fit does not seem to be stopping, or one fit follows another almost immediately. Most people with epilepsy who have tonic-clonic seizures recover completely from each fit within a very short time.

When the cause of epilepsy originates in one part of the brain, the seizures are called "partial". These fits may take the form of repeated movements of the hands or limbs. Lip smacking is quite common. The fit may be followed by a long period of confusion and odd behaviour. In schoolchildren this can often be thought to be a behavioural problem if epilepsy is not diagnosed. This type of epilepsy used to be called "temporal lobe epilepsy".

Sometimes people who have this type of fit experience a warning in the form of a particular taste or smell or other signal. This is called an "aura".

There are many types of epileptic fit, and every person has their own particular reaction to their fits. Doctors usually diagnose epilepsy after listening to their patient's (or the patient's parents') account of what has happened, as well as that of any reliable eye-witness. They may also ask the person to undergo certain tests which can help in the diagnosis.

Most people with epilepsy will have an E.E.G. test some time. This test records the electrical activity in the brain, using electrodes which are placed on the scalp. The test is painless, and sometimes shows an abnormal but characteristic pattern of activity which can help diagnose epilepsy. Many people who have fits only show abnormal patterns during the seizures, so this test is not a foolproof one, but it can help the doctor to decide which type of epilepsy a person has.

Another test which may be done is the C.T. scan. This produces a picture of the internal structure of the brain, and can show any structural damage which might have caused epilepsy. This might include brain damage or tumours.

Up to 80% of people with epilepsy can have their seizures abolished by using modern anti-epileptic drugs. Most of the others have the frequency and severity of their fits reduced by the drugs. These work by reducing the amount of electrical activity in the brain. Doctors have several drugs to choose from. For each patient, a doctor chooses a single drug as soon as the diagnosis has been made. The dosage of that drug is monitored using blood tests until control of fits has been achieved. If this does not happen, another drug is tried, until the best one at the best dosage has been found for that particular patient. Many drugs have side-effects, and so doctors use blood tests to monitor the effects of the drugs on their patients. Some people find that after they have been free from fits for a few years, they are able to reduce the amounts of drug they take and still remain free from fits.

When someone has been diagnosed as having epilepsy, they usually take some time to "come to terms" with the diagnosis. Parents find it difficult not to over protect their child, adults are frightened about something they do not understand. Most people come to terms with their epilepsy, but they worry about how other people will react. Society's attitude to epilepsy is improving, and families do not often regard one of their number with epilepsy as something to be ashamed of. People who have epilepsy can lead very normal lives in most cases as long as they take a few precautions. If their fits are controlled by drugs, then it is important to take them regularly, as prescribed. If their seizures are brought on by certain recognised things, such as TV or flashing lights, then these can be avoided. For children, it is important that their teachers and carers know what sort of fits they may have, and how to care for them. Other children, in the family and at school, may need to be reassured. This will help them to develop a caring and accepting attitude towards epilepsy. Most school activities are quite safe as long as there is good supervision.

People with epilepsy are allowed to drive a car, but only if they have been free from daytime-fits for two years or more. Epilepsy is not a great barrier to employment although the armed forces and police force do not accept people with epilepsy. Most other careers are open however, and local authorities have specialist careers officers who will help with advice.

Every day in the United Kingdom, about 80 people are told that they have epilepsy. The vast majority have their fits controlled, and lead very normal lives.

THE BRITISH EPILEPSY ASSOCIATION

The British Epilepsy Association (BEA) was founded to provide help and advice to people with epilepsy, their families and the professionals who work with them.

The BEA offers practical help through its professional counselling services and its network of self-help groups. It also offers legal advice and representation to people attending special appeals and industrial tribunals due to their epilepsy and will mediate in employer/employee misunderstandings about epilepsy. The BEA runs a special insurance scheme and holiday schemes for its members.

For many people with epilepsy, the most difficult problem they face is the social stigma still attached to epilepsy. To this end, the BEA's education department publishes information packs for schools and arranges conferences and seminars for both lay and professional audiences.

The BEA funds both medical and social research into epilepsy through the British Epilepsy Foundation.

If you require any information or would like a list of the comprehensive range of literature about all aspects of epilepsy which the BEA publishes, please contact
British Epilepsy Association
Anstey House
40 Hanover Square
Leeds LS8 BE

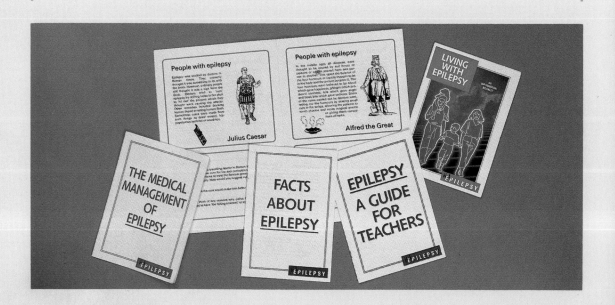

Glossary

Convulsion A violent, irregular movement of the limbs or whole body, caused by contraction of the muscles. The muscle contractions which cause convulsions are not under voluntary control, and can happen while the patient is unconscious.

C.T. scan C.T. stands for "Computerised Tomography." Tomography means displaying a picture of a slice through something. This technique builds up a picture of the inner structure of something, e.g. the brain, by processing a series of special X-rays of different planes throughout the organ. A computer analyses the X-ray information and presents it as a complex picture on a monitor screen.

E.E.G. This stands for "Electroencephalogram". The brain is an organ which has electrical activity in it. This can be detected if very sensitive electrodes are placed at different points on the scalp. The signal which is received by the electrodes is amplified and converted into a graph. Experienced doctors can interpret the patterns of these graphs and learn many things about the patient's condition. It is quite painless.

Migraine This is a condition from which many people suffer. It appears in many forms, but most people agree that the most common symptom is a severe headache.

Recovery position When a person is unconscious and can be moved safely, he or she should be put into the "recovery position." This entails rolling the person onto one side and arranging the arms and legs so that he or she will be comfortable and unlikely to roll into another position. Many people are sick when they come round. This sideways position makes sure that their airways remain clear and if they should be sick, that they will not inhale any fluids. A more detailed explanation of this technique will be found in any first-aid book.

Tonic-clonic "Tonic" means a continuous muscular contraction, and "clonic" means alternating muscular contractions and relaxations. Hence tonic-clonic seizures are those which are accompanied by the characteristic convulsions of epilepsy.

Reflex This is an involuntary reaction of the nervous system to an outside stimulus. The reaction happens automatically and independently of free will.

INDEX